www.finishinglinepress.com

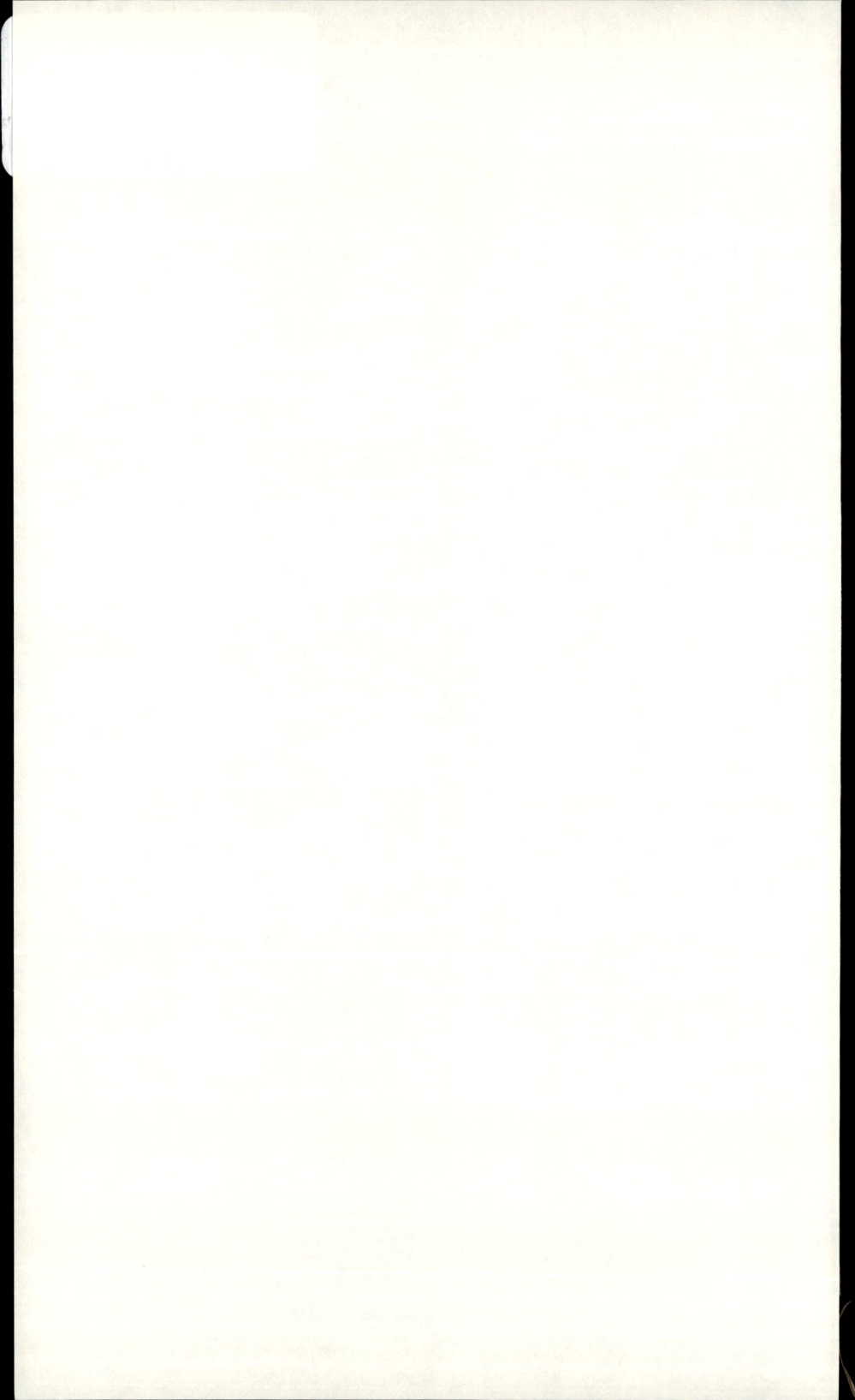

The Unreliable Narrator

poems by

C.M. Clark

Finishing Line Press
Georgetown, Kentucky

The Unreliable Narrator

ACKNOWLEDGMENTS

After Happy Hour Review: "Thyroid Insinuations & The Sandhill Cranes";
     "4 O'Clock in Old Bartow"; "The Cows Don't Care"
Bookends Review: "Tongue to Tarmac"
Pegasus: "Powerline Road & The White Butterflies"
Punt Volat (Barcelona): "World of Iron, World of Paper"
Vallum (Montreal): "Transplant of Marrow"
West Trade Review: "Next to Last Chance Saloon"
Wild Roof Journal: " Sky Dive at Sunrise"; "The Doula"

Publisher: Leah Huete de Maines
Editor: Christen Kincaid
Cover Art: "Shadow Work" by John Lunar Richey
Author Photo: C.M. Clark
Cover Design: Elizabeth Maines McCleavy

Order online: www.finishinglinepress.com
also available on amazon.com

Author inquiries and mail orders:
Finishing Line Press
PO Box 1626
Georgetown, Kentucky 40324
USA

Contents

For my boys of summer...
Julian Magnus
&
Calvin Andre

The Rhetoric of Fiction

It was that fulcrum time of day, the sigh surrendering
appetites and agendas. The signed armistice
that seeds your quiet. Your chill. How
to read these non-lines? A murder
of non-sequiturs? Crows on a wire. I
have seen it all before

and still hear the no-sound of pre-occupied breathing.
Is this how you will face
the foreshadowed future perfect
conjugated here in your shorthanded pause?
With an inconvenient stutter to shroud
the stale breakfast chatter,

the day's leylines and headlines? Is this
how it will come to become? The air unknowable
and still. And loud.
Hashmark footprints, whatever remains
of the sun, now mediated by duck blinds,
wood slats, performing their abacus of the hours.

What calculations do you foretell
in boldface integers on your screen?
Is this to be your lowest common denominator?
Your Rorschachs of bat, monster, first corsage?
As ever
I merely serve to see.

The unreliable narrator.

The Doula

This is a limited jurisdiction.
These are the paths that will host no guide. Will map
no hot turn around a crooked corner or
the narrow clearance on some blind mountain curve. Not meant

to prepare the waiting ground nor ease
the birth ridges that crease cartilage of ear folds or
calm ragged breath in a last crescendo
of gasp and cry, here at the first taste

of impossibly thin oxygen.

No, the doula's hands won't be turning
the face-up being being born, or
diagram the frontiers of transition, engines closing in
on overdrive.

No tensed hands here to measure, soothe reluctant tissue,
opening wide the jawbone folds, the plush ladies
in waiting. No, it will be the doula's ready tongue
that translates the huffed breath, whispers sweet nothings

into blood-fevered ears, reactivating the bits
of strength that blow wild
and go lost. No,

her hands will only appear
when words won't work, mobilizing instead just one
finger or two
to point the way.

The doula might be squeamish. She is reluctant
with skin. She is more about a look in the eye,
smoothing mangled pillow-hair, and she is loathe
to handle the bloody flux, the startling show,

probably hesitates even
to wipe a sweating face.

It would become my task to lull the static of dying. In waiting
to see prone feet in socks that seemed like my father's, thin
and down at the heel. Or perhaps remembered
from sifting through a bureau drawer like his, finding

the knit patterns favored by old men for old feet. This
was the time to invoke his household gods. That
is what the doula must do.

Somehow I was cast as the doula of dying
for him. Smoothed his manic brows,
crooned in a voice made for lullabies that sleep
would cure it all.

The doula is a woman servant, called as handmaiden to beginnings
and ends. A coach
on the sidelines somewhere at midfield, sometime
near midnight, to rant along the measured yards and call plays

without ever handling
the still round heart of the matter.

Remember how we swore to be midwives to each other?
Laying on the knowing hands to navigate
these perilous and ecstatic waters, narrow
channels between there and here?

But we ended up the doulas. Manhandling a tangle
of cables in roadside emergencies, reluctant,
resigned to kick-start
this now new and noise-cancelling normal

some call life.

Next to Last Chance Saloon

Halfway between cow and cormorant
Lake Wales appears. Your perfect excuse
to quit driving. To quit
the keener purpose of driving
between what is boundless and the finite. Always
the ground between.
An off-road shoulder like some old woman's bed
growing colder with years and indifferent. Can you imagine
the sheer acreage of exfoliating skin?

The body scent that fades
with each day's exhalation? Or are you called instead
inside a virtual elsewhere, the echoed jackhammer of feet
up
dizzying hexagons of tiled stairways?
Migraine-blind you rise
six flights. But the back bedroom stays hidden—
just waiting behind dry cleaning and winter coats
cocooned and swaddled in plastic. These

are the places that joust, that beckon
east to west, taking refuge and a lunch
where avoidance is most likely preferred
offering either
chicken fried steak or breakfast all day. Or
just the jazz
of numbing hours
and miles, just
for the lust of soft Gulf water.

There is a dead spot I like
between points on the map.
Still too close to the town receding
as only a vague blur of slow traffic
and low buildings fixed

in the rearview mirror. Yet
not yet near enough the next county line—
not yet my destination—yet a welcome
relief from the monotony
of brush and flat field.

In this dead spot I spin the dial.
Still a younger sister to radio days, knowing
the place by the cellphone towers.
Better than the billboards,
the come-to-Jesus vowels crooning

the oldies, the country quick nod
to God and Sunday.
But here
in the dead
spot

I snag only fragments of a place
already distant, and even fewer
half sentences anticipating
the next exit
still out beyond my windshield.

Straining to hear the transmissions
of forgettable voices straining
to assemble some meaningful
message, although every third word is swallowed
within the blur of road noise and wind shear.

From here to your front door due west
pavement plumbs the numbing miles.
The succinct limits of my very human vision—
my old tired eyes—the tired blue—succumbing
to cataract fog and still
straining west, the still unseen outpost
on your coast beyond my best attempt
to conjure you in your kitchen, closing
lower cupboards, with a brisk hip move.

The drawer with flatware juddered in closing,
hiding coupons, and lyrics to songs
that frame the stanzas of every evening's lullaby,
these late days left unsung. But
I hear it. Between waves.
Unseen
like the air.
Unflinching
like the sea.

World of Iron, World of Paper

It was to be the house on North Ola all over
again. Again with midnight intentions, you could walk
the seam that split
the north side from the one that grew

with the tax rolls. Sleepwalking along the attic's beams,
its wormhole abundance, the archived bulk of grocery lists,
floating invoices processed and deemed
seaworthy. The sheer ream weight

reverse engineering your vaginal birth, its mesmerizing
vestibule of ridged sidelights. It was the mirror
and the lamp
all over again.

A surprise move when you left
the blackened copies behind. Random
the past-sell-date of vegetables ordered. Medical services.
Provided. Pending. Land surveys and legal clauses

dividing one lot from another. The house would be
your arranged marriage. Its altar vows to caulk the gap while
the wood gleam sealed both sides
of an old incision, the troubling lacerations

brought to light in the yawning unsettling. And the center point.
The kitchen's hidden subfloor, waterways
iron and ancient. Rats' nests
hidden within steel wool.

The real entrance was scarcely used. Its postal address
on a different street, embroidered with leggy marigolds, sewn
on the bias, nearest the sidewalk. And the trellis only

visible when hit with seven spectrums of light, deep slats
pointless as shelter from rain or sun. Wild west outpost as entrance
or exit. Keyhole down an exhausted well.

By day you'd walk the planked oak between rooms. Invisible
this Maginot line between structures.
Trailing a loose hand that plagiarized wildly
and typed on erasable bond.

The old way.

It was a place you would come to wither and depart.
Somewhere you could walk out of, never crossing a bridge or
burning one. Never paying the ferryman's price or
giving him advice on how to steer or how to keep

his pole, his totem maintained.
How to salvage the rust prone, the medium of fade and dust.
Which carved faces of birds or gods would protect
or blame us. Offer solace. Sell sleep.

Barter for beads your fraudulent atonement.

Tongue to Tarmac

The third jump wakes the turtle, expatriate of the brackish backwater.
And when no one is watching, the tides—inch by inch,
neither salt nor fresh—erode my half acre. My half-life

spent sideswiping mile markers of gravel and tar
and spinning
spinning elliptically with inflated verve. Summoned

back not just to indentured space, but
slingshot to lace and latticework,
the familiar linens and pillows still holding

our heads' heat and indented shapes.
All trace evidence,
all reluctant keepsakes.

I am a planet again.

I remember closing time when the cabana boys appeared.
They would gather the sodden towels arch with sifted sand
and roll their rickshaws along the boardwalk. The day ceiling

would lift and the wind would jet, unstoppable.
It is last call at two.
Only time enough for bison on cave walls

and your two tanned legs counterpoised and
drawn from life—a virtual anatomy impossibly lithe
and life-like and fleet, but

no match
for the long
distance.

Draw the blinds.
Secure your cubicle,
your private metropolis of undress. Close

your mind, open your lips
and lip-sync
to the sing-song of earth's evening.

There is dust in this dwindling afternoon, and footprints.
The residue of planetary alignment. A particulate
afterburn that absorbs moisture and refracts

the light that's left. Give up, day.
Give up, won't you? Allow
all the voiced displeasures, the slouching torsos and clipped hair,

the plucked brows cluttering the aisles to exit.
They leave at last, the rusted trucks that clog
the avenues. They turn off side streets sooner than expected.

The vapor trail calls, tongue to tarmac.
Time
to circle back.

Who can imagine a wind like this? This
pulmonary therapy of pummeled oxygen?
The tight air has exhausted its gusto.

One last chance
to be
disqualified.

So far from the pulse
only a middle-aged star could offer,
I will lurch back along the known corridors.

Neighborhoods once familiar, or pre-determined or even
extra-sensory. The end result
the poorest translations, slang of a tone-deaf linguist

all quietly shelved, tucked into ramshackle files
intending impending loss. Lost
eventually, as the fingers of day workers dig

to find the misplaced molecules, the one iota
excised and held with surgical gloves and
poorly disguised distaste.

It is a tired and prodigal beckoning.
Some ways. All means.
No matter.

I am a planet again.

Powerline Road & The White Butterflies

It was controlled burn time in Indian River. A chore
of the moment, with no prior warning to take your lungs
inside. Inside your chest and beneath your skin—inside
where safe—at least, somewhat safe—or somewhere less
likely

to metastasize the ash of overgrown pine, scurrilous
palmetto,
charred shells of insects and young birds fallen
before their fledgling wings could
hope to hold the hollow bones

up.

Petals of ash floating like wedding bells pealing
in & on the breath, like will-less wishes
French braided, stunning choreographies paired
indistinguishably white

and only the white that is
smoked and back
lit. Just a fake
fall. More wishful thinking.

And only after the sun goes down,
you say, you promise, weighing
that pasteurized forgery, a false perception
on the western brink, here and now

escaping nimbus clouds'
confines. And so a circle's light
the hydrogen burns, still not moving except
to fire off redundant vapor,

wasteful
surplus
of matter. So technically
the sun doesn't go

down. But there is pleasure
in thinking it moves at our will at eyeblink speed aligning
with old narratives. Virtual
and unreal.

Stolen

from some calliope's painted face, there's not much
to weigh. What is familiar pushes front focused as far
as the street's limits. It is only late May. But

there's a sideshow staged anyway—with all roles played by the usual
    crew.
Unionized and anonymous, they flaunt catkin ribbons in a heady
    wind,
their frayed amulets. They'll unlikely remember

and they'll act done with this make-believe summer, dumb
and forgetting the humid hard afternoons, the hard months still
to come. So

they flit through kindergarten days relentless, their dwindling
    illusory.
A pantomime of sighing dusk,
the call to come inside and forget.

A hypocrite sun cooperates, stoneface jollying the pretense. An
    addict's
enabling the ever-longing of low latitudes for dark and summer's end.
But

for a summer waiting in the wings—
tutus all fluttering
more than likely—only virtual images

hover along the burnt edges of day. A fitting apparition—
more likely if, and only if, your ploughshares strike fool's gold.
A bloodless coup of false and mostly ever-cruel

fictions.

So, instead of peregrine ash, what floats becomes
winged, stylizing southward aboveground with the wires.
As long as they stay aloft, there are insect eyes and wills at work

all resplendent.
Off
they go.

The Safe House

There is safety in numbers and in the one webbed crook
where creped skin meets blue vein. Sometimes
sometime after the equinox every fall
as mullioned light

douses the inlaid table tops, lathe-turned chair legs,
where the indoor footfalls pause
and turn it all to honey, homebound
traffic heads west

stays where it belongs along
with the grumbled troubles that lie in neutral
and wait
their implacable turn. Stopped at the light

they hold off for the time being,
that time being just now. Mother may I
take just one deep breath held
in that solitary out of time,

since there is no longer the place
or occasion
where you can ask anyone
to be the mother today. Your shift

clocks out. Assembly line of drawn blinds,
pillows—sweet and laundered and beckoning—
fancy-free duvets in fashionable patterns, a no-name harbor
of the bright dark, land of the good dream quilt

outgrown.

Even the afternoon storms can insinuate shelter, if
the roof is snug, recently re-shingled. Tight
where heat-treated pine beams meet, nailed
not stapled, strap tied

for the duration. Tea
or a Swedish vodka cozily to toast
the company, the cats
hide beneath bed skirts, improvised hammocks and tucked

into soiled laundry in closet corners.

The safe room in the safe house is never showy.
The furniture is mismatched, often second-hand.
Where the baseboard meets the worn rug,
flattened weave of foot-traffic holds court. This

is the emblem of plain.
The antonym of celebrity. Never known
nor recognized, unsought and least likely
to broadcast

proof of life.

Sky Dive at Sunrise

This is the peril,
the rabid dog time. Out
of which quadrant of sky
will wet teeth snap?

Clear sight or a clean shot lurks just
beyond five outstretched fingertips. You
breathe out, the zero zen gasp held
ever since freefall. The parachute seems

to hold. You were told
not to twist, the blatant danger of strangle knot
or tangle of vital lines, but now
the urgency clutters your throat, swallowing

the rising sun. The day's oblique onset, its path shadowed
and foreshadowed. A new riddle,
more math
than mystery.

You assemble the brown mass of cows, the fields beneath fog
as cool dung and animal earth
first stir, the warmth of flesh opening
from sleep, dreams of food and shade and the forthcoming

turbulent young. Below, a coast road collates
oncoming traffic, separating
what remains stilled from
the grunt exhale of movement.

If an object falls free to earth
at 9.8 meters per second squared, how long
before you'd make contact with unforgiving ground?
Do the math! you nudge your invisible companions,

the indifferent vapors, the blinking,
unseeing eyes,
now insouciant and
sunstruck.

A pound of feathers and
a pound of lead, both descend.
One smelling of game bird, one
carcinogenic.

Twin equal signs,
indistinguishable
in the bead-blurred air,
the dull, coy clearing.

If the retina can separate
in a paroxysm of light's alarm—last burst
of unnamable glare and fleet object—
what seems sturdy and fixed, in fact

isn't. Do the math! you whisper still
a half mile above the rocky promontory. What
are the odds? What are my chances
to survive the textile collapse, the freefall

on a given Thursday morning early
in January? Catch as catch can the day's mandate:
the inevitable plummeting
to deaf acres, awash

in a sea of colored silk.

The Cows Don't Care

Now there are tadpoles and lily pads
floating, things surrounding
giving way to things
that precipitate and surface.

Mine weren't the arms
to cozy the new skin, hug hard
the bit-lip uncertainty
the hair-strand wonder.

Even

at a celebration, it was another's high laugh
juddering the imminent thunder, a sequined dress
spangles on water, short to the knees, the soft acquiescence
of bare legs and cocktail heels.

These

these were your bridesmaids, your consolation prize.
This so sketched and scheduled when
mine were not the hands
to hand you over.

Mine

sat in my lap, thunderstruck and hundreds of miles between
towers, another April morning outside Lake Wales
watching a cow chew, just twiddling a practiced pair
of useless and prehensile thumbs.

We

tiptoe around the sullen elegance like an itinerant mollusk
adding micrometer after micrometer of nacre
to a sand grain, cushioning the irritant—
an unintended, unvarnished

sore.

The cat mother's tongue smoothing
aligning the spacious valley
between eyes between
this and that, that virgin world

and

this on another hand, the one
that rocked the cradle, where sleeps the kingdom
of infant and innocence defined, its drain field
disintegrating without

ceremony.

Transplant of Marrow

Your cruel April begins in the dark where
there is still dark to these ends
of days. Still a blue evening, somewhere lilacs
still roosting with nesting creatures and
dishes resting in racks to dry.

Your dead-to-life April will last for the duration
of spring burgeoning. Am I up
to this task? Can there be sufficient
pauses
between synaptic links, torpedoes over the corpus

callosum, sufficient space
between there and beyond
to hold up my half. Let the month, the open mouth
do its work—your lips grim—
and I, I

I
will
do
mine.

Of course, she left
no carbon footprint. Her feet
were made of lead.

The lead barricades shielding
her chest from dental x-rays caught
decay in rear molars, suspicion

of further erosion of gum and
the last teeth to cut, but
shields can only shield

so much. Her heart beneath
her chest knew the lead from early
on. Knew where it originated

where the dumb barrier discovered
its ground.
The gamma pulses pierced

anyway. She stored the messages
as data. To see her
as a pioneer of ecological promise

was a system error. Carbon no longer, now
she feasts with the silicone gossips
that surround her encampment.

Circling the wagons, so to
speak.

4 O'Clock in Old Bartow

Solid, deep blue and eager for her brokenness,
Mary Orsini wrote more checks than receipts
by the time the moon bit down. More
absence notes than permission slips. More
consonants than vowels. Her pen

itched.

I suppose I should mention
the solar eclipse, she thought.
That
at least would ground the day
and link the slice of moon

over sun to one given year
and point as surely to the candle's color,
its lavender trajectory. The ounce
or two of Chardonnay left lukewarm
in someone's cup. The night falsified

its hour clocked equally by town crier
or blind owl seeing
only the dregs
of jasmine, this premature
and fraudulent dark. It seems the change

started earlier elsewhere. Eyes protected we
can only hope to chamois the humid skies
of moisture, insistent reminders of a season
that just
won't

surrender.

There.

It's come on us early,
this extraordinary afternoon's elongations,
sidewalk shadows aping encephalitic skulls,
like alien fingers
of one hand, arthritic and

clapping.

I

will bring the other hand forward
to reach an amalgam of pixels
so familiar, so cousin-like. So soon
we will meet
at the already groaning board.

What

she asks, can I bring to this already laden supper,
what will hosts offer up only
when all blinds are drawn,
the tilted lattice slats
shut. The recalcitrant young

walk the neighborhood,
their hair unfalteringly
long, predictably
brown. She was
tired of the trees' flowers,

the flowering.

As daylight

time returned to these dull latitudes,
the breath hush settled. No glory or lull
this afternoon, late sun gone early
behind western cloud hills and
appetite lost

for movement. Things
and cells settle alike,
shouldering for their share of space
and pre-occupied air. The light escapes
with the fumes of drying paint.

It is Salome's dance, this exhale
of a quenched candle. Once a head on a plate
noticed only in its absence, neither
missing
nor mourning

the spent hot wax.

Thyroid Insinuations & The Sandhill Cranes

It was before she saw the dunes and the paved roadways,
the symphony of zippers that give way, electrifying
twin concrete lanes cracked
in the corners, sugared with sand, and as sure

as magnetic poles rule the longitude line from Greenwich
mean to a gated mews facing 60 West,
the silvered teeth snap shut, clacking their reluctant closure,
now a soldered wound overheated and healed, but only

for now.

Such simpering, the bored diagnosis. Adamant to trust
those calculations of enzyme and excess, triglyceride
pressure quotients, the drip
drip

drip of aortal determination. Better try
elsewhere with your stents, the
calipers and speculums always colder
than promised. It's

just a small gland, like others
pocketing their endocrine rhythms in secret
adherence to a lodestar, a set of mirrored instructions
as yet

unencrypted.

She remembers the katydid calls
and who can resist? A voice
that falls
into the soprano's cleaved register. But

along the curve
as the road curls west and away
from the known cleared lots, also in their time
silenced by concrete's slump and pour,

never wasting one peck
or one misplaced feather, their slender necks—
uninterrupted—lean like sand dune grasses, waiting
without hope.

Just a seamless blur
in their massed grouping,
the collective stubbornness imitating
what passes in some circles

for hunger.

The Hermit Crab

I am no mollusk nor mollusk
lover, Mary told all
who could hear the snaps and
surges of self-scrutiny. Her time

alone sagged and stretched these days with stasis
as their instrument, their agency. Her time
in the sun, the cool of winter
the miles that unfolded all the way west.

The midpoint was singular and shifting. Some trips
it was the gas station that bloomed out—
flat reaches of flat fields and two-lane roads
where passing zones came suddenly

and necessary. In April
the bugs blurred
her road view, a hailstorm
of copulating bodies and juices

free fall, flash flood. Frenzied wipers could do nothing
to keep up. Negotiating the cheapened airpockets
of Osceola County, they retreated. Twelve
plagues, fat frogs and locusts

and the Israelites were released.

C.M. Clark's work has appeared throughout the U.S., in Canada, and internationally. Publication credits include *Painted Bride Quarterly, West Trade Review, Wild Roof Journal, Bookends Review, Prime Number Magazine, Vallum Magazine* (Montreal), *Punt Volat* (Barcelona), *The Paddock Review, Pegasus, Ovenbird,* and the *South Florida Poetry Journal.* Her work has been anthologized in collections including Anhinga Press's *Rumors, Secrets and Lies,* Demeter Press's *Travellin' Mama,* in *Voices from the Fierce Intangible World* (South Florida Poetry Journal Annual), and in *Chasing Light* (Yellow Jacket Press). Clark was a finalist for the Anhinga Press 2021 Chapbook Prize, and runner-up for the Slate Roof Press Elyse Wolf Prize. Clark is the author of full-length works *Exoskeletal* (Solution Hole Press, 2019), *Dragonfly* (Solution Hole Press, 2016), *Charles Deering Forecasts the Weather & Other Poems* (Solution Hole Press, 2012), *The Blue Hour* (Three Stars Press, 2007), *Pillow Talk,* a collaboration with painter Georges LeBar (Porky Pie Press, 2007), as well as the chapbook, *The Five Snouts,* (Finishing Line Press, 2017).

Clark continues to collaborate with artists from other media, including a partnership with contemporary composer Andres Carrizo; a video project, "String Theory," (featured in a corollary exhibit to Miami's Art Basel) with painter Georges LeBar; and Miami's SWEAT Broadside Project, with artists Dorothy Simpson Krause and Kim Yantis. She also served as inaugural Poet-in-Residence for the Deering Estate Artists Village in Miami, and has been featured in programs on contemporary American poetry at the Miami Book Fair.

www.ingramcontent.com/pod-product-compliance
Lightning Source LLC
Chambersburg PA
CBHW022057080426
42734CB00009B/1391